INTERMEDIARIES

NVOCC & FREIGHT FORWARDING

DEVARAJAN THYAGARAJAN

DEDICATED TO MY FAMILY PRIYA DEVARAJAN,SHARATH DEVARAJAN,JANANI DEVARAJAN AND MY PARENTS

Facilitator : Shipper to Carrier & Carrier to Shipper for the movement of cargoes from Point A to Point B

NVOCC

Non-Vessel Owning Common Carriers, NVOCC are Shipping companies/Logistics Service providers that organize shipments for their clients 'independently' i.e.

- The company doesn't own any vessels.
- It issues its **bill of lading (B/L or BoL)**.

It signs contracts with Liner companies to transport containers and goods. An NVOCC leases space from other ocean carriers (or VOCCs). They act as an intermediary, responsible and accountable for sales, stuffing, and transportation of the cargo, Collection of freight, and other charges from point A to B.

The NVOCC companies function as ocean carriers but without operating the vessel. However, they often need clarification from the freight forwarders.

ROLL OF NVOCC

- They issue the House Bill of Lading
- Apart from operational costs, NVOCC may add a profit percentage after leasing the space from carriers.
- NVOCC acts as an Intermediary. I.e. Carrier to Shippers and Shipper to Carriers.
- NVOCCs can own a fleet of containers.
- NVOCC helps small and medium businesses that may only require part of their container to ship their goods. NVOCCs lease or rent space in containers from large shippers or freight forwarders, and sell it to smaller shippers.

NVOCC LICENSE and ITS IMPORTANCE:

- Non-US-based companies may get registered with FMC. (Federal Maritime Commission). But it is not mandatory.
- In India, NVOCCs are regulated by DGS. (Director General of Shipping)
- Having an FMC license means NVOCCs can negotiate deals with the shipping lines. It authorizes or allows to rise House Bill of Lading which is considered a carrier bill.

NVOCC AGGREGATOR MARKET: LEADING REGIONS*

- North Americal(US, Canada & Mexico)
- Europe(UK,Germany,France, Italy, Russia,Turkey)
- Asia Pacific(India,China,Japan, Korea,Australia)
- South America(Argentina, Brazil, Columbia, etc.)
- ME and Africa(Saudi Arabia, UAR,Egypt,Nigeria & South Africa)

* Source : Market Research report

Importance of FMC License

- Right Pricing

  FMC prevents NVOCCs from charging customers unfair costs by monitoring agreements, including mergers and acquisitions among the carriers.

- Regulations

  FMC license regulates everything for NVOCCs. That gives you as a shipper some security. Because when working with an FMC-licensed NVOCC shippers have someplace to go if they need help with unfair treatment.

- Reliability

  Shippers prefer to work with FMC-licensed NVOCC because it provides a safety net. Many things can happen with the

NVOCC. It can go out of business, or any other damage occurs while having the shippers' cargo in their possession.

NVOCC: MAJOR CHALLENGES

- Blank sailings
- Trip cancellations
- Right size capacity
- Declining market demand
- Container shortage

NVOCC: AUTOMATION & DIGITIZATION :

KEY DRIVING FACTORS

Cloud computing :

- NVOCC aggregators totally depend on IT solutions to improve the security, efficiency, and dependability of shipping operations, that's where Cloud computing plays a vital role.

- Predominantly Cloud computing assists NVOCC aggregators in optimizing the utilization of information resources

- Cloud computing serves as the Saas (Software as a service)model for Shipping industries particularly in the area of fleet management, Documentation management, maintenance management, and the status of the ships or fleets.

IoT and Smart tracking

- The use of smart container tracking insights is giving the NVOCC aggregators the predictive insights they need to manage container allocation effectively.

- NVOCC aggregators can better track containers and receive data via online smart tracking using IoT (Internet of Things) devices. This allows them to improve fleet allocation and better match supply with shipper demand.

- IoT devices send out real-time alerts to shippers as to their products, arriving/departing at a port, etc.

NVOCCs: TASKS

- Issues Bill of Lading or House Bill of Lading
- Responsible and accountable for moving cargo from Customers to the gateway ports
- Consulting and Process of documents
- Handling Warehouse and First/last mile deliveries
- Negotiating contracts and other shipping-related tariffs such customs, port, etc.
- Handling of cargo and Transportation activities.

NVOCC: MARKET STRATEGY

- Analyze the shipping industry in India in depth and the competitors.
- Understand Market trends
- Customer demands
- Competitive landscape
- Segmentation based on Cargoes, Shipping routes, and customer needs.
- USP should be clear in terms of competitive pricing, Customer service & niche specialization.
- Volume-based discount for customers with large shipments.
- Comprehensive Marketing Plan
- Business presence online, Networking with Liners and shippers.
- Implement and close monitoring of CRM(Customer Relationship Management)
- Ensure customers are engaged fully and excellent service levels are maintained.
- Digitization like Cloud computing, IoT, Track and trace, SAAS, etc.
- Ensure to get contiguous feedback from the customer and take necessary steps immediately.
- Ensure legal and regulatory compliance.

- Ensure that the business complies with all shipping and trade regulations to build trust with customers.
- Last, but not least regularly review the strategy and make corrections

NVOCC IN INDIA: STARTUP: OUTLINE

- Identify specific and Target Markets within the shipping industry
- Understand service offerings when intend to provide
- Prepare a detailed Business plan, which includes Business objectives, Budget, Marketing strategy, and SOP.
- Registration and Licensing: A necessary license needs to be obtained from DG Shipping.
- Contiguous Relationship with the Liners and the shipping fraternity.
- Invest in Infra: Either purchase or lease containers, whichever is economical.
- Optimum utilization of resources and effective utilization of spaces.
- Implementing IT/Digitization in terms of managing bookings, Documentation track and trace, etc. Creating technology interfaces with shipping lines, ports, and customers can streamline operational efficiency.
- Marketing and Sales Strategy play a vital role in terms of

pulling customers on board.

- ⬤ Ensure all statutory, legal, Maritime law, Service Tax, International agreements, Insurance, and regulation adherence have been followed.

- ⬤ NVOCC business needs to be registered under the Companies Act and obtain a Permanent Account number.

- ⬤ SWOT analysis of competitors and the market.

- ⬤ Data analytics: It can provide insights into market trends, customer behavior, and operational efficiency.

NVOCC CHARGES:

NVOCC charges vary from port to port and it may depend on the carrier. Common NVOCC charges are ;

- ⬤ Terminal Handling charges
- ⬤ Seal Charges
- ⬤ BL Charges
- ⬤ Delivery Order charges
- ⬤ Survey Charges
- ⬤ Cleaning and Washing Charges

TOP NVOCC PLAYERS IN INDIA

- ECU Worldwide India
- Kintesu Worl Express
- DHL Global Forwarding
- NNR Global Logistics
- Schenker India
- Kuene +Nagel
- Expeditors International
- Damco
- Agility/DSV
- CMA CGM
- Panalpina World Transport
- SML Group
- DHL eCommerce
- Far East Organization
- Maersk Line
- Sinotrans
- FedEx Trade Networks
- JAS Forwarding
- Transworld Group
- APL
- K line
- OOCL
- Hamburg Sud India
- Hapag-Llyod
- NYK Line

- Simatech Shipping
- Caravel
- C.H.Robinson

SUMMARY:

The aforementioned specific aspects are crucial for successfully starting an NVOCC in India. Ensure Business complies with all legal requirements, stands strong in the competitive landscape, manages costs effectively, and leverages technology for maximum efficiency.

FREIGHT FORWARDING

A Freight forwarder is a company that acts as an intermediary between multimodal transport companies that import and export goods and the businesses that need them. They do not own anything but facilitate in terms of moving goods from point A to point B.

As middlemen between the business making the shipment and

the final destination of the products, freight forwarders are essential to the supply chain. They offer a variety of modes, including road transport, rail freight, air freight, sea/ocean freight, Warehousing, customs clearance, etc., even if they do not handle the shipments directly. They frequently carry a single shipment using several modes.

FREIGHT FORWARDING: GLOBAL MARKET SIZE*

The market for freight forwarding was estimated to be worth USD 200.98 billion in 2022, and between 2023 and 2030, it is projected to expand at a compound annual growth rate(CAGR) of 4.6%.

Globalization has been a major factor in the market's expansion.

*Source: Market research report

FREIGHT AND LOGISTICS MARKET SIZE: INDIA*

The India freight and logistics market size is estimated at 288.18 billion USD in 2023 and is expected to reach 484.43 billion USD by 2029, growing at a CAGR of 9.04% during the forecast period 2023-2029.

*Source: Market research report

FREIGHT FORWARDER: PRIMARY RESPONSIBILITIES

- Documentation for Importing or exporting goods
- Selecting the right mode of transportation to move cargo to their destination.
- Negotiating freight chargers with the Liners/Multimodal/ LSPs
- Consolidating freight for the shipments.
- Inventory management
- Insurance, wherever it is required.

FREIGHT FORWARDING: PROCESS

Freight Forwarding Process

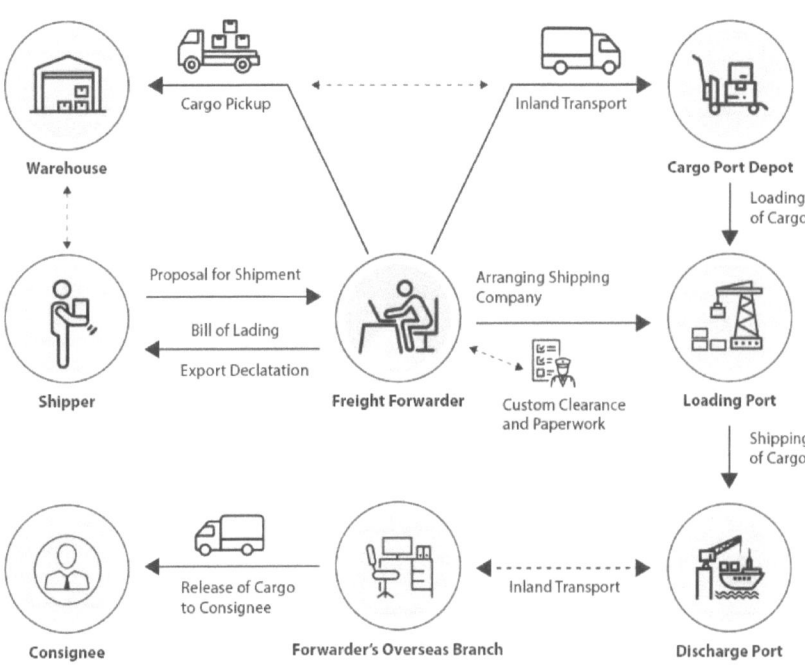

The freight forwarding process involves end-to-end supply chain management. It involves

- Export Haulage

- Export Customs clearance
- Inland Transportation at Origin
- Origin/Terminal Handling
- Import/Terminal Handling
- Import haulage
- Inland Transportation at Destination
- Container freight station
- Import Customs clearance
- Destination Arrival and Handling
- Last mile deliveries

EXPORT HAULAGE:

- The first stage of freight forwarding is to pick up cargo from the Manufacturer's/Factory/Shipper's premise
- Movement of Cargoes from the Shipper's premise to the Freight forwarder's warehouse.
- Selection of the right transport is very crucial depending on the company's cargoes and the distance to the freight forwarder's warehouse.

EXPORT CUSTOMS CLEARANCE:

- Cargoes are moved to Container freight station for Customs clearance.
- At the Container freight station, Cargoes are being inspected to make sure they arrived without damage and confirm that they match the booking documents for the order.
- The freight forwarding team also checks to ensure that the destination point will accept the shipment.
- Cargoes are offloaded at the Container freight station, in Export Warehouse.
- Certain items like Flammable liquids, drugs, alcohol, Dangerous items, perishable items etc, may have restrictions, particularly if they are going to a country other than their country of origin. Needs to be checked thoroughly.
- Necessary documentation is being done.
- Customs official does Assessment and Examination.
- A trailer is being arranged and empty containers are being picked from the liner's plot.
- Stuffing permission is given by customs officials, once the documents are perfect.
- Once stuffing is completed, Customs officials do due diligence, examination, and "Let export Order"(LEO) being given.
- Custom officials also validate the safety and legality of the cargo before allowing it to leave the country.
- For the above activities, normally Freight forwarders hire a

Licensed Customs broker to handle the "Clearance process".

IMPORT CUSTOMS CLEARANCE

- On receipt of cargo at the destination country, authorities check the necessary documentation being provided by the Freight forwarder, which may include: Invoices, Bill of lading certificate, Export packing list, license and declaration document, Certificate of origin, Inspection certificate, etc.
- They ensure that products are meeting the legal requirements for entry into the country.
- Import CHAs do all paperwork and move the cargo to the Destination Container freight station(nominated by the customer).
- At the Container freight station, Cargoes are offloaded, and Customs clearance is given in terms "Out of Charge"(OOC).
- Cargoes are either moved from CFS to the Shipper's end location point or Destuffed at the Container freight station, depending upon the end customer's choice.

IMPORT HAULAGE

The last phase of the process is Import haulage, where cargoes are moved from the Container freight Station's import warehouse to the final destination point. The final destination point may be located at Local or in the Upcountry, depending upon the location, and suitable transportation being arranged, which is called **"Last Mile Deliveries"**.

NEED FOR FREIGHT FORWARDER!

- Shipping larger orders from a business is made easier with the help of freight forwarders, especially when those orders are being transported to other countries.
- They get the required papers and insurance, offer the shipper storage and warehousing options, and keep their clients updated on the status of each shipment.
- By giving businesses a single invoice for all services rendered, freight forwarders simplify the process of managing freight or businesses.
- End customers are being benefited as Freight forwarders are managing their "end to end movements" as a single point contact, thereby customers to focus on increasing their Core productivity and revenues.

FREIGHT FORWARDERS:

TARGET SEGMENT INDUSTRIES

- Manufacturing
- E Commerce
- Electrical and Electronics
- FMCG
- Reefer
- Food
- RMG(Readymade Garments)
- Textile/Yarn
- Chemicals
- Steels
- Paper
- Timber logs
- Pharma
- Machinery
- Auto CKDs/SKDs

SETTING UP FREIGHT FORWARDING INDUSTRY

IN INDIA: OUTLOOK

Introduction/Background:

The Indian freight forwarding business has excellent potential due to rising domestic production activity and consumption trends, as well as increasing interaction with the global economy.

For example, in FY 2021-22, India's import volume increased to US$610 billion* while its exports totaled US$417.8 billion*. Such high numbers support the market's need for logistics and are a sign of a substantial amount of trade that involves India. This has made it possible for the "freight forwarding" sector in India to flourish.

Supply chain distribution is outsourced to intermediates as big businesses now seek to concentrate on their core competencies.

As a result, there is a need for freight forwarders, who can do their jobs very affordably. Furthermore, the logistics and supply chain industry in India is undergoing a major transformation, modernization, and infrastructure development due to factors like:

- Growing Digitization

- Shifting consumer preferences
- Growth of eCommerce
- Supportive Government policies like the PM Gati Shakti Yojna, National Asset Monetization pipeline, National Logistics Policy(NLP), etc.

*Source: Market research

DOCUMENTS REQUIRED BY THE FREIGHT FORWARDER:

- Commercial Invoice
- Packing List
- Export Shipping bill
- Certificate of Orgin
- Letter of Credit(if applicable)
- Insurance certificate
- Bill of Lading
- Declaration of Haz cargo

FREIGHT FORWARDING UNIT: SETING UP IN INDIA:

The following important steps are to be kept in mind , while setting up a freight forwarding unit in India.

- Business model
- Register for statutory licenses/mandatory compliances
- Landscape regulatory

BUSINESS MODEL:

The first and foremost is to decide what business structures are suited, whether it is

- Sole Proprietorship
- Partnership firm'
- Limited Liability Partnership(LLP)
- Private Limited company
- Public Limited company
- One Person Company(OPC)

REGISTER FOR STATUTORY LICENSES/ MANDATORY COMPLIANCES

In India, a freight forwarder is governed by the following statutes:

- **MTO:** Multimodal Transportation of goods, Act, 1993

- **Carriage of Goods:** There are 3 categories, namely
  1. Land: Carriage by Road Act, 2007
  Carriage by Rail, The Railways Act, 1989

- **Sea:** The Indian Bills of Lading Act, 1856
  The Carriage of Goods by Sea Act, 1925
  The Merchant Shipping Act, 1958
  The Marine Insurance Act, 1963

- **Air:** The Carriage by Air Act, 1972

Warehousing:
The Warehousing (Development and Regulation) Act, 2007

National Logistics Policy(NLP):

The Logistics industry has got momentum through the PM Gati Shakti program to ease the supply chain bottlenecks and expedite the development of an integrated logistics ecosystem in Inda. Its implemented to reduce the overall logistics cost.

INCOTERMS:

Incoterms are nothing but a set of rules for International trade. It defines the responsibilities of sellers and buyers.

Incoterms specify who is responsible and accountable for paying for managing the shipment, Insurance, documentation, customs clearance and other logistics-associated activities.

Incoterms are decided by the International Chamber of Commerce, located in France.

Some of the frequent Incoterms used by the customers are as follows:

ExW (Ex Works):

Buyer's(Importer) responsibility from the Source to destination.

FOB(Free on Board):

The buyer's (Importer) responsibility starts from Ocean freight to till he gets good.

Seller's(Exporter) responsibility is Origin trucking, Terminal handling and Customs.

CIF: Cost , Insurance and Freight, the seller covers the CIF of a buyer's order while in transit.

DDP: Delivered Duty Paid: Seller's(Exporter) responsibility from Door to Door

DDU: Delivered Duty Unpaid: Seller(Exporter) will deliver the goods as soon as they are made available at an agreed-upon location in the country to which they are imported. The buyer (Importer) needs to take care of duties, fees, etc.

SHIPPER'S EXPECTATION:

- Shipper's need for customization
- Guaranteed prices & loading capacity
- Consolidated invoicing
- Robust and rigid re-liability requirements between different parties involved in transportation
- Need for involvement of many different types of parties in shipments
- Ambidextrous capabilities and digital forwarder talents

FREIGHT FORWARDING : ANALOG VS DIGITAL

ANALOG:

Shipper   Intermediary FF   Carreier

Forwarding Contract   Carriage of Contract

DIGITAL:

Direct Interactions

Shipper   Carrier

Affiliat

Platform

DIGITAL FORWARDERS:

- Shippers are encouraged to entrust digital forwarders with their goods by offering a selling pitch that includes invoice consolidation, pricing stability, assured capacity, and liability.

- Large clients and complicated traffic flows can benefit from the tailored solutions that freight forwarders can provide, as long as important functions like capacity brokerage, routing, and pricing are handled by people.This will allow small clients with sporadic, simple

  shipments and without complex customs management to be serviced easily.

- These digital forwarders are going to be preferred partners. Once special advantage of digital freight forwarders is their capacity to integrate both poles of governance in their intermediary platform.

- On the one hand, they offer quality – liability and trust, while on the other they also offer quantity – proprietary hubs, domestic shipments, and a network of tens of thousands of carriers in multiple countries.

Few of the top Freight forwarding players uses Digital platform:

MAERSK: Alibaba's **"One touch Platform"** to allow

shippers

to directly book "Vessel Capacity" online.

DHL: DHL uses **"SALOODO"** platform: It connecrts shippers

with FTL/LTL carriers in Europe and elsewhere.

KUENE+NAGHEL : **"Freight -Net Patform"** provides binding

Carrier quotations, Direct booking, Online track and trace etc.

FREIGHT FORWARDING INDUSTRY:

FRAGMENTED STRUCTURE*

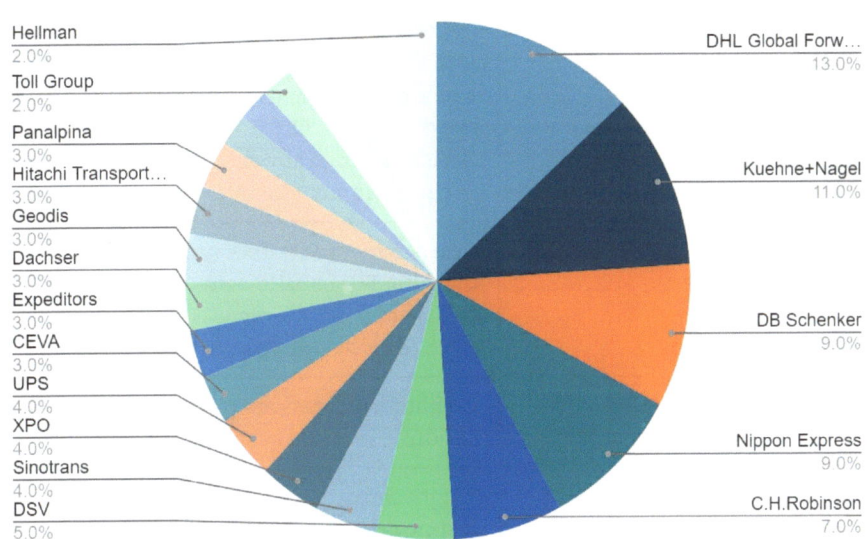

Hellman 2.0%	DHL Global Forw... 13.0%
Toll Group 2.0%	Kuehne+Nagel 11.0%
Panalpina 3.0%	DB Schenker 9.0%
Hitachi Transport... 3.0%	Nippon Express 9.0%
Geodis 3.0%	C.H.Robinson 7.0%
Dachser 3.0%	
Expeditors 3.0%	
CEVA 3.0%	
UPS 4.0%	
XPO 4.0%	
Sinotrans 4.0%	
DSV 5.0%	

*Market research report

43

DIFFERENCE BETWEEN NVOCC AND FREIGHT FORWARDING

NVOCC	FREIGHT FORWARDING
NVOCCs issue the House Bill of Lading.NVOCCs operate independently and do not belong to any international organization.	Freight forwarders issue a BL in accordance with International Federation of Freight forwarders Associations(FIATA) documents standarization. BLs are issued by individual carriers arranged by the freight forwarder on the customer's behalf.
NVOCC does not own Vessel, but owning Containers.	Freight forwarders does not own anything.But usually owns or leases a warehouse for storage.The freight forwarders do not operate the containers.
NVOCCs are permitted to add a profit margin for their services.	Freight forwarders are permitted to add Handling fees and other surcharges.
NVOCCs have agreements with the shipping lines and also with the shippers, and hence act as a mediator between both parties.	Freight forwarders represent shippers while dealing with the shipping lines.
NVOCCs accept full legal responsibility for goods they are shipping in the event of loss or damage,	Legal responsibility for goods is with the individual carrier being used to transport the goods, not the freight forwarder.
The NVOCC operates	Freight forwarders from different world

independently and determines the tariffs themselves	countries are networked and together discuss costs and ways to improve deliveries.
Ocean transport Intermediaries	Ocean transport Intermediaries
NVOCCs act as a carrier to shippers and a shipper to the carriers.	Freight forwarders acts as an agent for the shipper.

OCEAN FREIGHT:

- **Pre-Carriage** – The movement that happens **BEFORE** the container is loaded on the ocean going vessel
- **Carriage** – The movement that happens while the container is **ON BOARD** the ship
- **On-Carriage** – The movement that happens **AFTER** the container is discharged from the ocean going vessel

Pre-Carriage – It is the term given to the movement that takes place prior to the container being loaded at a port of loading on to an ocean going vessel.. Such activity can take place at the same location as the port of loading, or at a location close to the port of loading..

This activity is known as **PRE-CARRIAGE**..

If the activity is performed by the shipping line on behalf of the client, that movement is called Carrier Haulage..

In a Carrier's haulage, this activity can be performed by the carrier using rail, road, inland waterways transport or multimodal.

If the activity is performed by the client or their transporter, that is called Merchant Haulage.. This activity can be performed using rail, or road transport..

Carriage – is the term given to the movement of the cargo by sea from the port of load to the port of discharge..

This activity is known as **CARRIAGE**..

This activity can be performed only by the shipping line/vessel operator who is undertaking to carry the cargo from point A to point B and the bill of lading issued by the ship owner/shipping line is the evidence of the contract of such carriage..

On-Carriage – is the term given to any movement that takes place after the container is discharged at a port of discharge from the ocean going vessel..

GLOABAL MAJOR SHIPPING TRADE LANES:

- Asia -US
- Asia-Europe
- Europe-UK
- North America-Canada
- Intra-Asia

ASIA-US

The Panama Canal facilitates major trade between Asia and the US. This is one of the most strategically built ma-made shipping lanes in the world.

ASIA-EUROPE

The Suez Canal facilitates direct trade link between Asia and Europe, around 19000 ships travelled on this 193K/m route on average, representing 12% of the Global trade and 30% of global container traffic.

EUROPE -UK

The Dover Strait, making it an important trade link between Europe and UK.This route is one of thebusinest maritime routes globaqlly, handling an estimate of 400 commercial vessels daily,.

NORTH AMERICA-CANADA

The St.Lawrence Seaway ,facilitates shipping between American and Canadian waters, specifically upper parts of Canada.This route is the focal point of American and Canadian international trade.The seaway handles 40-50 million tons of cargo annually, comprising iron ore, grains, mining products, liquid bulk etc.

INTRA-ASIA

The Strait of Malacca, forming the main and the largest passageway between the Indian Ocean and the Pacific Ocean, is a major shipping lane into and out of Asia.It connects India, China and Japan to each other and other important asian countries such as Thailand, Indonesia, Malaysia, Philippines, Singapore, Vietnam,Taiwan,and South Korea.making it an important arterial shipping lane in the world. Handling around 50000 Vessels per year , which contributes one -quarter of the World's sea trade.

IMPORTANT SEA ROUTES :

ALONG MAJOR WORLD TRADE LANES:

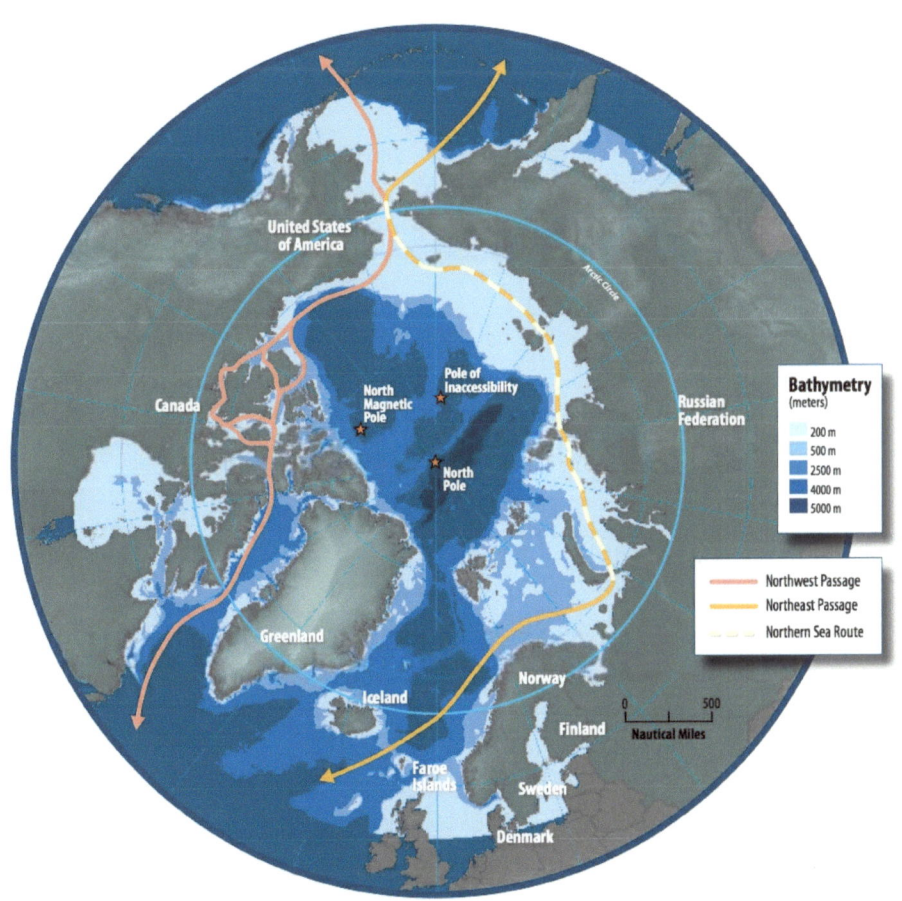

- The English Channel
- Strait of Malacca
- Panama Canal
- Suez Canal
- The South and East China seas
- Strait of Hormuz
- Strait of Gibraltar
- The Danish Straits
- St.Lawrence Seaway
- Bosphorus Strait

ABOUT THE AUTHOR

Devarajan Thyagarajan

Devarajan is an astute business-oriented leader with a career spanning around 3 decades in Logistics and Supply chain management. Having rich leadership experience and worked with various large Corporations and MNCs with the capacity of CEO, Director, and Vice President. Almost 30 years have been involved in Leading, Managing, and Delivering Supply chain and Logistics activities for various clientele across the verticals. I'm a passionate fitness enthusiast and a dedicated business leader, committed to pursuing excellence in both arenas. My journey is a testament to the power of discipline, hard work, and a relentless pursuit of personal and professional growth. Born and raised with a deep love for sports (Cricket & table tennis) and physical fitness, my journey into the world of fitness began at a young age. As I honed my physical prowess, I recognized the importance of discipline and goal-setting, skills that would serve well in the Business world.

On the Education front, Devarajan holds a triple Post Graduates namely MA, MBA., PGDMM (Materials Management), a Diploma in Export Management in Marine, and EDP in Supply Chain Management from IIT Delhi.

In the realm of business, I embarked on a career filled with challenges and opportunities. Over the years, I climbed the corporate ladder, learning invaluable lessons about leadership, teamwork, and strategic decision-making. My commitment to personal growth and leadership led me to various leadership roles within organizations, where I had the privilege of shaping teams and driving success.

My true calling, however, remained in the fitness industry. I decided to combine my passion for fitness with my business acumen, launched my own fitness brand 'HIFI FITNESS STUDIO'. Through perseverance and a dedication, am treating Logistics & SCM as well as Fitness as integral part of myself. All mile stones were achieved sheer support from my family, without that I would not have reached where I am.

BOOKS BY THIS AUTHOR

How To Get Succeeded In Job Interview

Proven ways to get desired jobs!

3Pl (Third Party Logistics)

All about Warehousing, Value added services and Last mile deliviers

Container Freight Station(Cfs)

All about Container freight station

www.ingramcontent.com/pod-product-compliance
Lightning Source LLC
Chambersburg PA
CBHW050830290526
45792CB00001B/334